The Biography of a Grizzly / The Trail of the Sandhill Stag (annotated)

by

Ernest Thompson Seton

Author of: Wild Animals I Have Known; Art Anatomy of Animals; Mammals of Manitoba; Birds of Manitoba

PART I

THE CUBHOOD OF WAHB

He was born over a score of years ago, away up in the wildest part of the wild West, on the head of the Little Piney, above where the Palette Ranch is now.

His Mother was just an ordinary Silvertip, living the quiet life that all Bears prefer, minding her own business and doing her duty by her family, asking no favors of any one excepting to let her alone. It was July before she took her remarkable family down the Little Piney to the Graybull, and showed them what strawberries were, and where to find them.

Notwithstanding their Mother's deep conviction, the cubs were not remarkably big or bright; yet they were a remarkable family, for there were four of them, and it is not often a Grizzly Mother can boast of more than two.

The woolly-coated little creatures were having a fine time, and reveled in the lovely mountain summer and the abundance of good things. Their Mother turned over each log and flat stone they came to, and the moment it was lifted they all rushed under it like a lot of little pigs to lick up the ants and grubs there hidden.

It never once occurred to them that Mammy's strength might fail sometime, and let the great rock drop just as they got under it; nor would any one have thought so that might have chanced to see that huge arm and that shoulder sliding about under the great yellow robe she wore. No, no; that arm could never fail. The little ones were quite right. So they hustled and tumbled one another at each fresh log in their haste to be first, and squealed little squeals, and growled little growls, as if each was a pig, a pup, and a kitten all rolled into one.

They were well acquainted with the common little brown ants that harbor under logs in the uplands, but now they came for the first time on one of the hills of the great, fat, luscious Wood-ant, and they all crowded around to lick up those that ran out. But they soon found that they were licking up more cactus-prickles and sand than ants, till their Mother said in Grizzly, "Let me show you how."

She knocked off the top of the hill, then laid her great paw flat on it for a few moments, and as the angry ants swarmed on to it she licked them up with one lick, and got a good rich mouthful to crunch, without a grain of sand or a cactus-stinger in it. The cubs soon learned. Each put up both his little brown paws, so that there was a ring of paws all around the ant-hill, and there they sat, like children playing 'hands,' and each licked first the right and then the left paw, or one cuffed his brother's ears for licking a paw that was not his own, till the ant-hill was cleared out and they were ready for a change.

Ants are sour food and made the Bears thirsty, so the old one led down to the river. After they had drunk as much as they wanted, and dabbled their feet, they walked down the bank to a pool, where the old one's keen eye caught sight of a number of Buffalo-fish basking on the bottom. The water was very low, mere pebbly rapids between these deep holes, so Mammy said to the little ones:

"Now you all sit there on the bank and learn something new."

First she went to the lower end of the pool and stirred up a cloud of mud which hung in the still water, and sent a long tail floating like a curtain over the rapids just below. Then she went quietly round by land, and sprang into the upper end of the pool with all the noise she could. The fish had crowded to that end, but this sudden attack sent them off in a panic, and they dashed blindly into the mud-cloud. Out of fifty fish there is always a good chance of some being fools, and half a dozen of these dashed through the darkened water into the current, and before they knew it they were struggling over the shingly shallow. The old Grizzly jerked them out to the bank, and the little ones rushed noisily on these funny, short snakes that could not get away, and gobbled and gorged till their little bellies looked like balloons.

They had eaten so much now, and the sun was so hot, that all were quite sleepy. So the Mother-bear led them to a quiet little nook, and as soon as she lay down, though they were puffing with heat, they all snuggled around her and went to sleep, with their little brown paws curled in, and their little black noses tucked into their wool as though it were a very cold day.

After an hour or two they began to yawn and stretch themselves, except little Fuzz, the smallest; she poked out her sharp nose for a moment, then snuggled back between her Mother's great arms, for she was a gentle, petted little thing. The largest, the one afterward known as Wahb, sprawled over on his back and began to worry a root that stuck up, grumbling to himself as he chewed it, or slapped it with his paw for not staying where he wanted it. Presently Mooney, the mischief, began tugging at Frizzle's ears, and got his own well boxed. They clenched for a tussle; then, locked in a tight, little grizzly yellow ball, they sprawled over and over on the grass, and, before they knew it, down a bank, and away out of sight toward the river.

Almost immediately there was an outcry of yells for help from the little wrestlers. There could be no mistaking the real terror in their voices. Some dreadful danger was threatening.

Up jumped the gentle Mother, changed into a perfect demon, and over the bank in time to see a huge Range-bull make a deadly charge at what he doubtless took for a yellow dog. In a moment all would have been over with Frizzle, for he had missed his footing on the bank; but there was a thumping of heavy feet, a roar that startled even the great Bull, and, like a huge bounding ball of yellow fur, Mother Grizzly was upon him. Him! the monarch of the herd, the master of all these plains, what had he to fear? He bellowed his deep war-cry, and charged to pin the old one to the bank; but as he bent to tear her with his shining horns, she dealt him a stunning blow, and before he could recover she was on his shoulders, raking the flesh from his ribs with sweep after sweep of her terrific claws.

The Bull roared with rage, and plunged and reared, dragging Mother Grizzly with him; then, as he hurled heavily off the slope, she let go to save herself, and the Bull rolled down into the river.

This was a lucky thing for him, for the Grizzly did not want to follow him there; so he waded out on the other side, and bellowing with fury and pain, slunk off to join the herd to which he belonged.

II.

Old Colonel Pickett, the cattle king, was out riding the range. The night before, he had seen the new moon descending over the white cone of Pickett's Peak.

"I saw the last moon over Frank's Peak," said he, "and the luck was against me for a month; now I reckon it's my turn."

Next morning his luck began. A letter came from Washington granting his request that a post-office be established at his ranch, and contained the polite inquiry, "What name do you suggest for the new post-office?"

The Colonel took down his new rifle, a 45-90 repeater. "May as well," he said; "this is my month"; and he rode up the Graybull to see how the cattle were doing.

As he passed under the Rimrock Mountain he heard a far-away roaring as of Bulls fighting, but thought nothing of it till he rounded the point and saw on the flat below a lot of his cattle pawing the dust and bellowing as they always do when they smell the blood of one of their number. He soon saw that the great Bull, 'the boss of the bunch,' was covered with blood. His back and sides were torn as by a Mountain-lion, and his head was battered as by another Bull.

"Grizzly," growled the Colonel, for he knew the mountains. He quickly noted the general direction of the Bull's back trail, then rode toward a high bank that offered a view. This was across the gravelly ford of the Graybull, near the mouth of the Piney. His horse splashed through the cold water and began jerkily to climb the other bank.

As soon as the rider's head rose above the bank his hand grabbed the rifle, for there in full sight were five Grizzly Bears, an old one and four cubs. "Run for the woods," growled the Mother Grizzly, for she knew that men carried guns. Not that she feared for herself; but the idea of such things among her darlings was too horrible to think of. She set off to guide them to the timber-tangle on the Lower Piney. But an awful, murderous fusillade began.

Bang! and Mother Grizzly felt a deadly pang.

Bang! and poor little Fuzz rolled over with a scream of pain and lay still.

With a roar of hate and fury Mother Grizzly turned to attack the enemy.

Bang! and she fell paralyzed and dying with a high shoulder shot. And the three little cubs, not knowing what to do, ran back to their Mother.

Bang! bang! and Mooney and Frizzle sank in dying agonies beside her, and Wahb, terrified and stupefied, ran in a circle about them. Then, hardly knowing why, he turned and dashed into the timber-tangle, and disappeared as a last bang left him with a stinging pain and a useless, broken hind paw.

* * * * *

That is why the post-office was called Four-Bears. The Colonel seemed pleased with what he had done; indeed, he told of it himself.

But away up in the woods of Anderson's Peak that night a little lame Grizzly might have been seen wandering, limping along, leaving a bloody spot each time he tried to set down his hind paw; whining and whimpering, "Mother! Mother! Oh, Mother, where are you?" for he was cold and hungry, and had such a pain in his foot. But there was no Mother to come to him, and he dared not go back where he had left her, so he wandered aimlessly about among the pines.

Then he smelled some strange animal smell and heard heavy footsteps; and not knowing what else to do, he climbed a tree. Presently a band of great, long-necked, slim-legged animals, taller than his Mother, came by under the tree. He had seen such once before and had not been afraid of them then, because he had been with his Mother. But now he kept very quiet in the tree, and the big creatures stopped picking the grass when they were near him, and blowing their noses, ran out of sight.

He stayed in the tree till near morning, and then he was so stiff with cold that he could scarcely get down. But the warm sun came up, and he felt better as he sought about for berries and ants, for he was very hungry. Then he went back to the Piney and put his wounded foot in the ice-cold water.

He wanted to get back to the mountains again, but still he felt he must go to where he had left his Mother and brothers. When the afternoon grew warm, he went limping down the stream through the timber, and down on the banks of the Graybull till he came to the place where yesterday they had had the fish-feast; and he eagerly crunched the heads and remains that he found. But there was an odd and horrid smell on the wind. It frightened him, and as he went down to where he last had seen his Mother the smell grew worse. He peeped out cautiously at the place, and saw there a lot of Coyotes, tearing at something. What it was he did not know; but he saw no

Mother, and the smell that sickened and terrified him was worse than ever, so he quietly turned back toward the timber-tangle of the Lower Piney, and nevermore came back to look for his lost family. He wanted his Mother as much as ever, but something told him it was no use.

As cold night came down, he missed her more and more again, and he whimpered as he limped along, a miserable, lonely, little, motherless Bear- -not lost in the mountains, for he had no home to seek, but so sick and lonely, and with such a pain in his foot, and in his stomach a craving for the drink that would nevermore be his. That night he found a hollow log, and crawling in, he tried to dream that his Mother's great, furry arms were around him, and he snuffled himself to sleep.

III.

Wahb had always been a gloomy little Bear; and the string of misfortunes that came on him just as his mind was forming made him more than ever sullen and morose. It seemed as though every one were against him. He tried to keep out of sight in the upper woods of the Piney, seeking his food by day and resting at night in the hollow log. But one evening he found it occupied by a Porcupine as big as himself and as bad as a cactus-bush. Wahb could do nothing with him. He had to give up the log and seek another nest.

One day he went down on the Graybull flat to dig some roots that his Mother had taught him were good. But before he had well begun, a grayish-looking animal came out of a hole in the ground and rushed at him, hissing and growling. Wahb did not know it was a Badger, but he saw it was a fierce animal as big as himself. He was sick, and lame too, so he limped away and never stopped till he was on a ridge in the next canyon. Here a Coyote saw him, and came bounding after him, calling at the same time to another to come and join the fun. Wahb was near a tree, so he scrambled up to the branches. The Coyotes came bounding and yelping below, but their noses told them that this was a young Grizzly they had chased, and they soon decided that a young Grizzly in a tree means a Mother Grizzly not far away, and they had better let him alone.

After they had sneaked off Wahb came down and returned to the Piney. There was better feeding on the Graybull, but every one seemed against him there now that his loving guardian was gone, while on the Piney he had peace at least sometimes, and there were plenty of trees that he could climb when an enemy came.

His broken foot was a long time in healing; indeed, it never got quite well. The wound healed and the soreness wore off, but it left a stiffness that gave him a slight limp, and the sole-balls grew together quite unlike those of the other foot. It particularly annoyed him when he had to climb a tree or run fast from his enemies; and of them he found no end, though never once did a friend cross his path. When he lost his Mother he lost his best and only friend. She would have taught him much that he had to learn by bitter experience, and would have saved him from most of the ills that befell him in his cubhood--ills so many and so dire that but for his native sturdiness he never could have passed through alive.

The pines bore plentifully that year, and the winds began to shower down the ripe, rich nuts. Life was becoming a little easier for Wahb. He was gaining in health and strength, and the creatures he daily met now let him alone. But as he feasted on the pines one morning after a gale, a great Black-bear came marching down the hill. 'No one meets a friend in the woods,' was a byword that Wahb had learned already. He swung up the nearest tree. At first the Black-bear was scared, for he smelled the smell of Grizzly; but when he saw it was only a cub, he took courage and came growling at Wahb. He could climb as well as the little Grizzly, or better, and high as Wahb went, the Blackbear followed, and when Wahb got out on the smallest and highest twig that would carry him, the Blackbear cruelly shook him off, so that he was thrown to the ground, bruised and shaken and half-stunned. He limped away moaning, and the only thing that kept the Blackbear from following him up and perhaps killing him was the fear that the old Grizzly might be about. So Wahb was driven away down the creek from all the good woods.

There was not much food on the Graybull now. The berries were nearly all gone; there were no fish or ants to get, and Wahb, hurt, lonely, and miserable, wandered on and on, till he was away down toward the Meteetsee. A Coyote came bounding and barking through the sage-brush after him. Wahb tried to run, but it was no use; the Coyote was soon up with him. Then with a sudden rush of desperate courage Wahb turned and charged his foe. The astonished Coyote gave a scared yowl or two, and fled with his tail between his legs. Thus Wahb learned that war is the price of peace.

But the forage was poor here; there were too many cattle; and Wahb was making for a far-away woods in the Meteetsee Canyon when he saw a man, just like the one he had seen on that day of sorrow. At the same moment he heard a bang, and some sage-brush rattled and fell just over his back. All the dreadful smells and dangers of that day came back to his memory, and Wahb ran as he never had run before.

He soon got into a gully and followed it into the canyon. An opening between two cliffs seemed to offer shelter, but as he ran toward it a Range-cow came trotting between, shaking her head at him and snorting threats against his life.

He leaped aside upon a long log that led up a bank, but at once a savage Bobcat appeared on the other end and warned him to go back. It was no time to quarrel. Bitterly Wahb felt that the world was full of enemies. But he turned and scrambled up a rocky bank into the woods that border the benches of the Meteetsee.

The Pine Squirrels seemed to resent his coming, and barked furiously. They were thinking about their nuts. They knew that this Bear was coming to steal their provisions, and they followed him overhead to scold and abuse him, with such an outcry that an enemy might have followed him by their noise, which was exactly what they intended.

There was no one following, but it made Wahb uneasy and nervous. So he kept on till he reached the timber line, where both food and foes were scarce, and here on the edge of the Mountain-sheep land at last he got a chance to rest.

IV.

Wahb never was sweet-tempered like his baby sister, and the persecutions by his numerous foes were making him more and more sour. Why could not they let him alone in his misery? Why was every one against him? If only he had his Mother back! If he could only have killed that Black-bear that had driven him from his woods! It did not occur to him that some day he himself would be big. And that spiteful Bobcat, that took advantage of him; and the man that had tried to kill him. He did not forget any of them, and he hated them all.

Wahb found his new range fairly good, because it was a good nut year. He learned just what the Squirrels feared he would, for his nose directed him to the little granaries where they had stored up great quantities of nuts for winter's use. It was hard on the Squirrels, but it was good luck for Wahb, for the nuts were delicious food. And when the days shortened and the nights began to be frosty, he had grown fat and well-favored.

He traveled over all parts of the canyon now, living mostly in the higher woods, but coming down at times to forage almost as far as the river. One night as he wandered by the deep-water a peculiar smell reached his nose. It was quite pleasant, so he followed it up to the water's edge. It seemed to come from a sunken log. As he reached over toward this, there was a sudden clank, and one of his paws was caught in a strong, steel Beaver-trap.

Wahb yelled and jerked back with all his strength, and tore up the stake that held the trap. He tried to shake it off, then ran away through the bushes trailing it. He tore at it with his teeth; but there it hung, quiet, cold, strong, and immovable. Every little while he tore at it with his teeth and claws, or beat it against the ground. He buried it in the earth, then climbed a low tree, hoping to leave it behind; but still it clung, biting into his flesh. He made for his own woods, and sat down to try to puzzle it out. He did not know what it was, but his little green-brown eyes glared with a mixture of pain, fright, and fury as he tried to understand his new enemy.

He lay down under the bushes, and, intent on deliberately crushing the thing, he held it down with one paw while he tightened his teeth on the other end, and bearing down as it slid away, the trap jaws opened and the foot was free. It was mere chance, of course, that led him to squeeze both springs at once. He did not understand it, but he did not forget it, and he got these not very clear ideas: 'There is a dreadful little enemy that hides by the water and waits for one. It has an odd smell. It bites one's paws and is too hard for one to bite. But it can be got off by hard squeezing.'

For a week or more the little Grizzly had another sore paw, but it was not very bad if he did not do any climbing.

It was now the season when the Elk were bugling on the mountains. Wahb heard them all night, and once or twice had to climb to get away from one of the big-antlered Bulls. It was also the season when the trappers were coming into the mountains, and the Wild Geese were honking overhead. There were several quite new smells in the woods, too. Wahb followed one of these up, and it led to a place where were some small logs piled together; then, mixed with the smell that had drawn him, was one that he hated--he remembered it from the time when he had lost his Mother. He sniffed about carefully, for it was not very strong, and learned that this hateful smell was on a log in front, and the sweet smell that made his mouth water was under some brush behind. So he went around, pulled away the brush till he got the prize, a piece of meat, and as he grabbed it, the log in front went down with a heavy chock. It made Wahb jump; but he got away all right with the meat and some new ideas, and with one old idea made stronger, and that was, 'When that hateful smell is around it always means trouble.'

As the weather grew colder, Wahb became very sleepy; he slept all day when it was frosty. He had not any fixed place to sleep in; he knew a number of dry ledges for sunny weather, and one or two sheltered nooks for stormy days. He had a very comfortable nest under a root, and one day, as it began to blow and snow, he crawled into this and curled up to sleep. The storm howled without. The snow fell deeper and deeper. It draped the pine-trees till they bowed, then shook themselves clear to be draped anew. It drifted over the mountains and poured down the funnel-like ravines, blowing off the peaks and ridges, and filling up the hollows level with their rims. It piled up over Wahb's den, shutting out the cold of the winter, shutting out itself: and Wahb slept and slept.

V.

He slept all winter without waking, for such is the way of Bears, and yet when spring came and aroused him, he knew that he had been asleep a long time. He was not much changed--he had grown in height, and yet was but little thinner. He was now very hungry, and forcing his way through the deep drift that still lay over his den, he set out to look for food. There were no nuts to get, and no berries or ants; but Wahb's nose led him away up the canyon to the body of a winter-killed Elk, where he had a fine feast, and then buried the rest for future use.

Day after day he came back till he had finished it. Food was very scarce for a couple of months, and after the Elk was eaten, Wahb lost all the fat he had when he awoke. One day he climbed over the Divide into the Warhouse Valley. It was warm and sunny there, vegetation was well advanced, and he found good forage. He wandered down toward the thick timber, and soon smelled the smell of another Grizzly. This grew stronger and led him to a single tree by a Bear-trail. Wahb reared up on his hind feet to smell this tree. It was strong of Bear, and was plastered with mud and Grizzly hair far higher, than he could reach; and Wahb knew that it must have been a very large Bear that had rubbed himself there. He felt uneasy. He used to long to meet one of his own kind, yet now that there was a chance of it he was filled with dread.

No one had shown him anything but hatred in his lonely, unprotected life, and he could not tell what this older Bear might do. As he stood in doubt, he caught sight of the old Grizzly himself slouching along a hillside, stopping from time to time to dig up the quamash-roots and wild turnips.

He was a monster. Wahb instinctively distrusted him, and sneaked away through the woods and up a rocky bluff where he could watch.

Then the big fellow came on Wahb's track and rumbled a deep growl of anger; he followed the trail to the tree, and rearing up, he tore the bark with his claws, far above where Wahb had reached. Then he strode rapidly along Wahb's trail. But the cub had seen enough. He fled back over the Divide into the Meteetsee Canyon, and realized in his dim, bearish way that he was at peace there because the Bear-forage was so poor.

As the summer came on, his coat was shed. His skin got very itchy, and he found pleasure in rolling in the mud and scraping his back against some convenient tree. He never climbed now: his claws were too long, and his arms, though growing big and strong, were losing that suppleness of wrist that makes cub Grizzlies and all Blackbears great climbers. He now dropped naturally into the Bear habit of seeing how high he could reach with his nose on the rubbing-post, whenever he was near one.

He may not have noticed it, yet each time he came to a post, after a week or two away, he could reach higher, for Wahb was growing fast and coming into his strength.

Sometimes he was at one end of the country that he felt was his, and sometimes at another, but he had frequent use for the rubbing-tree, and thus it was that his range was mapped out by posts with his own mark on them.

One day late in summer he sighted a stranger on his land, a glossy Blackbear, and he felt furious against the interloper. As the Blackbear came nearer Wahb noticed the tan-red face, the white spot on his breast, and then the bit out of his ear, and last of all the wind brought a whiff. There could be no further doubt; it was the very smell: this was the black coward that had chased him down the Piney long ago. But how he had shrunken! Before, he had looked like a giant; now Wahb felt he could crush him with one paw. Revenge is sweet, Wahb felt, though he did not exactly say it, and he went for that red-nosed Bear. But the Black one went up a small tree like a Squirrel. Wahb tried to follow as the other once followed him, but somehow he could not. He did not seem to know how to take hold now, and after a while he gave it up and went away, although the Blackbear brought him back more than once by coughing in derision. Later on that day, when the Grizzly passed again, the red-nosed one had gone.

As the summer waned, the upper forage-grounds began to give out, and Wahb ventured down to the Lower Meteetsee one night to explore. There was a pleasant odor on the breeze, and following it up, Wahb came to the carcass of a Steer. A good distance away from it were some tiny Coyotes, mere dwarfs compared with those he remembered. Right by the carcass was another that jumped about in the moonlight in a foolish way. For some strange reason it seemed unable to get away. Wahb's old hatred broke out. He rushed up. In a flash the Coyote bit him several times before, with one blow of that great paw, Wahb smashed him into a limp, furry rag; then broke in all his ribs with a crunch or two of his jaws. Oh, but it was good to feel the hot, bloody juices oozing between his teeth!

The Coyote was caught in a trap. Wahb hated the smell of the iron, so he went to the other side of the carcass, where it was not so strong, and had eaten but little before clank, and his foot was caught in a Wolf-trap that he had not seen.

But he remembered that he had once before been caught and had escaped by squeezing the trap. He set a hind foot on each spring and pressed till the trap opened and released his paw. About the carcass was the smell that he knew stood for man, so he left it and wandered down-stream; but more and more often he got whiffs of that horrible odor, so he turned and went back to his quiet benches. Wahb's third summer had brought him the stature of a large-sized Bear, though not nearly the bulk and power that in time were his. He was very light-colored now, and this was why Spahwat, a Shoshone Indian who more than once hunted him, called him the Whitebear, or Wahb.

Spahwat was a good hunter, and as soon as he saw the rubbing-tree on the Upper Meteetsee he knew that he was on the range of a big Grizzly. He bushwhacked the whole valley, and spent many days before he found a chance to shoot; then Wahb got a stinging flesh-wound in the shoulder. He growled horribly, but it had seemed to take the fight out of him; he scrambled up the valley and over the lower hills till he reached a quiet haunt, where he lay down.

His knowledge of healing was wholly instinctive. He licked the wound and all around it, and sought to be quiet. The licking removed the dirt, and by massage reduced the inflammation, and it plastered the hair down as a sort of dressing over the wound to keep out the air, dirt, and microbes. There could be no better treatment.

But the Indian was on his trail. Before long the smell warned Wahb that a foe was coming, so he quietly climbed farther up the mountain to another resting-place. But again he sensed the Indian's approach, and made off. Several times this happened, and at length there was a second shot and another galling wound. Wahb was furious now. There was nothing that really frightened him but that horrible odor of man, iron, and guns, that he remembered from the day when he lost his Mother; but now all fear of these left him. He heaved painfully up the mountain again, and along under a six-foot ledge, then up and back to the top of the bank, where he lay flat. On came the Indian, armed with knife and gun; deftly, swiftly keeping on the trail; floating joyfully over each bloody print that meant such anguish to the hunted Bear. Straight up the slide of broken rock he came, where Wahb, ferocious with pain, was waiting on the ledge. On sneaked the dogged hunter; his eye still scanned the bloody slots or swept the woods ahead, but never was raised to glance above the ledge. And Wahb, as he saw this shape of Death relentless on his track, and smelled the hated smell, poised his bulk at heavy cost upon his quivering, mangled arm, there held until the proper instant came, then to his sound arm's matchless native force he added all the weight of desperate hate as down he struck one fearful, crushing blow. The Indian sank without a cry, and then dropped out of sight. Wahb rose, and sought again a quiet nook where he might nurse his wounds. Thus he learned that one must fight for peace; for he never saw that Indian again, and he had time to rest and recover.

PART II

I.

The years went on as before, except that each winter Wahb slept less soundly, and each spring he came out earlier and was a bigger Grizzly, with fewer enemies that dared to face him. When his sixth year came he was a very big, strong, sullen Bear, with neither friendship nor love in his life since that evil day on the Lower Piney.

No one ever heard of Wahb's mate. No one believes that he ever had one. The love-season of Bears came and went year after year, but left him alone in his prime as he had been in his youth. It is not good for a Bear to be alone; it is bad for him in every way. His habitual moroseness grew with his strength, and any one chancing to meet him now would have called him a dangerous Grizzly.

He had lived in the Meteetsee Valley since first he betook himself there, and his character had been shaped by many little adventures with traps and his wild rivals of the mountains. But there was none of the latter that he now feared, and he knew enough to avoid the first, for that penetrating odor of man and iron was a never-failing warning, especially after an experience which befell him in his sixth year.

His ever-reliable nose told him that there was a dead Elk down among the timber.

He went up the wind, and there, sure enough, was the great delicious carcass, already torn open at the very best place. True, there was that terrible man-and-iron taint, but it was so slight and the feast so tempting that after circling around and inspecting the carcass from his eight feet of stature, as he stood erect, he went cautiously forward, and at once was caught by his left paw in an enormous Bear-trap. He roared with pain and slashed about in a fury. But this was no Beaver-trap; it was a big forty-pound Bear-catcher, and he was surely caught.

Wahb fairly foamed with rage, and madly grit his teeth upon the trap. Then he remembered his former experiences. He placed the trap between his hind legs, with a hind paw on each spring, and pressed down with all his weight. But it was not enough. He dragged off the trap and its clog, and went clanking up the mountain. Again and again he tried to free his foot, but in vain, till he came where a great trunk crossed the trail a few feet from the ground. By chance, or happy thought, he reared again under this and made a new attempt. With a hind foot on each spring and his mighty shoulders underneath the tree, he bore down with his titanic strength: the great steel springs gave way, the jaws relaxed, and he tore out his foot. So Wahb was free again, though he left behind a great toe which had been nearly severed by the first snap of the steel.

Again Wahb had a painful wound to nurse, and as he was a left-handed Bear,--that is, when he wished to turn a rock over he stood on the right paw and turned with the left,--one result of this disablement was to rob him for a time of all those dainty foods that are found under rocks or logs. The wound healed at last, but he never forgot that experience, and thenceforth the pungent smell of man and iron, even without the gun smell, never failed to enrage him.

Many experiences had taught him that it is better to run if he only smelled the hunter or heard him far away, but to fight desperately if the man was close at hand. And the cow-boys soon came to know that the Upper Meteetsee was the range of a Bear that was better let alone.

II.

One day after a long absence Wahb came into the lower part of his range, and saw to his surprise one of the wooden dens that men make for themselves. As he came around to get the wind, he sensed the taint that never failed to infuriate him now, and a moment later he heard a loud bang and felt a stinging shock in his left hind leg, the old stiff leg. He wheeled about, in time to see a man running toward the new-made shanty. Had the shot been in his shoulder Wahb would have been helpless, but it was not.

Mighty arms that could toss pine logs like broomsticks, paws that with one tap could crush the biggest Bull upon the range, claws that could tear huge slabs of rock from the mountain-side--what was even the deadly rifle to them!

When the man's partner came home that night he found him on the reddened shanty floor. The bloody trail from outside and a shaky, scribbled note on the back of a paper novel told the tale.

It was Wahb done it. I seen him by the spring and wounded him. I tried to git on the shanty, but he ketched me. My God, how I suffer! JACK. It was all fair. The man had invaded the Bear's country, had tried to take the Bear's life, and had lost his own. But Jack's partner swore he would kill that Bear.

He took up the trail and followed it up the canyon, and there bushwhacked and hunted day after day. He put out baits and traps, and at length one day he heard a crash, clatter, thump, and a huge rock bounded down a bank into a wood, scaring out a couple of deer that floated away like thistle-down. Miller thought at first that it was a land-slide; but he soon knew that it was Wahb that had rolled the boulder over merely for the sake of two or three ants beneath it.

The wind had not betrayed him, so on peering through the bush Miller saw the great Bear as he fed, favoring his left hind leg and growling sullenly to himself at a fresh twinge of pain. Miller steadied himself, and thought, "Here goes a finisher or a dead miss." He gave a sharp whistle, the Bear stopped every move, and, as he stood with ears acock, the man fired at his head.

But at that moment the great shaggy head moved, only an infuriating scratch was given, the smoke betrayed the man's place, and the Grizzly made savage, three-legged haste to catch his foe.

Miller dropped his gun and swung lightly into a tree, the only large one near. Wahb raged in vain against the trunk. He tore off the bark with his teeth and claws; but Miller was safe beyond his reach. For fully four hours the Grizzly watched, then gave it up, and slowly went off into the bushes till lost to view. Miller watched him from the tree, and afterward waited nearly an hour to be sure that the Bear was gone. He then slipped to the ground, got his gun, and set out for camp. But Wahb was cunning; he had only seemed to go away, and then had sneaked back quietly to watch. As soon as the man was away from the tree, too far to return, Wahb dashed after him. In spite of his wounds the Bear could move the faster. Within a quarter of a mile--well, Wahb did just what the man had sworn to do to him.

Long afterward his friends found the gun and enough to tell the tale.

The claim-shanty on the Meteetsee fell to pieces. It never again was used, for no man cared to enter a country that had but few allurements to offset its evident curse of ill luck, and where such a terrible Grizzly was always on the war-path.

III.

Then they found good gold on the Upper Meteetsee. Miners came in pairs and wandered through the peaks, rooting up the ground and spoiling the little streams--grizzly old men mostly, that had lived their lives in the mountain and were themselves slowly turning into Grizzly Bears; digging and grubbing everywhere, not for good, wholesome roots, but for that shiny yellow sand that they could not eat; living the lives of Grizzlies, asking nothing but to be let alone to dig.

They seemed to understand Grizzly Wahb. The first time they met, Wahb reared up on his hind legs, and the wicked green lightnings began to twinkle in his small eyes. The elder man said to his mate:

"Let him alone, and he won't bother you."

"Ain't he an awful size, though?" replied the other, nervously.

Wahb was about to charge, but something held him back--a something that had no reference to his senses, that was felt only when they were still; a something that in Bear and Man is wiser than his wisdom, and that points the way at every doubtful fork in the dim and winding trail.

Of course Wahb did not understand what the men said, but he did feel that there was something different here. The smell of man and iron was there, but not of that maddening kind, and he missed the pungent odor that even yet brought back the dark days of his cubhood.

The men did not move, so Wahb rumbled a subterranean growl, dropped down on his four feet, and went on.

Late the same year Wahb ran across the red-nosed Blackbear. How that Bear did keep on shrinking! Wahb could have hurled him across the Graybull with one tap now.

But the Blackbear did not mean to let him try. He hustled his fat, podgy body up a tree at a rate that made him puff. Wahb reached up nine feet from the ground, and with one rake of his huge claws tore off the bark clear to the shining white wood and down nearly to the ground; and the Blackbear shivered and whimpered with terror as the scraping of those awful claws ran up the trunk and up his spine in a way that was horribly suggestive.

What was it that the sight of that Blackbear stirred in Wahb? Was it memories of the Upper Piney, long forgotten; thoughts of a woodland rich in food?

Wahb left him trembling up there as high as he could get, and without any very clear purpose swung along the upper benches of the Meteetsee down to the Graybull, around the foot of the Rimrock Mountain; on, till hours later he found himself in the timber-tangle of the Lower Piney, and among the berries and ants of the old times.

He had forgotten what a fine land the Piney was: plenty of food, no miners to spoil the streams, no hunters to keep an eye on, and no mosquitos or flies, but plenty of open, sunny glades and sheltering woods, backed up by high, straight cliffs to turn the colder winds. There were, moreover, no resident Grizzlies, no signs even of passing travelers, and the Blackbears that were in possession did not count.

Wahb was well pleased. He rolled his vast bulk in an old Buffalo-wallow, and rearing up against a tree where the Piney Canyon quits the Graybull Canyon, he left on it his mark fully eight feet from the ground.

In the days that followed he wandered farther and farther up among the rugged spurs of the Shoshones, and took possession as he went. He found the signboards of several Blackbears, and if they were small dead trees he sent them crashing to earth with a drive of his giant paw. If they were green, he put his own mark over the other mark, and made it clearer by slashing the bark with the great pickaxes that grew on his toes.

The Upper Piney had so long been a Blackbear range that the Squirrels had ceased storing their harvest in hollow trees, and were now using the spaces under flat rocks, where the Blackbears could not get at them; so Wahb found this a land of plenty: every fourth or fifth rock in the pine woods was the roof of a Squirrel or Chipmunk granary, and when he turned it over, if the little owner were there, Wahb did not scruple to flatten him with his paw and devour him as an agreeable relish to his own provisions. And wherever Wahb went he put up his sign-board:

Trespassers beware!

It was written on the trees as high up as he could reach, and every one that came by understood that the scent of it and the hair in it were those of the great Grizzly Wahb.

If his Mother had lived to train him, Wahb would have known that a good range in spring may be a bad one in summer. Wahb found out by years of experience that a total change with the seasons is best. In the early spring the Cattle and Elk ranges, with their winter-killed carcasses, offer a bountiful feast. In early summer the best forage is on the warm hill-sides where the quamash and the Indian turnip grow. In late summer the berry-bushes along the river-flat are laden with fruit, and in autumn the pine woods gave good chances to fatten for the winter. So he added to his range each year. He not only cleared out the Blackbears from the Piney and the Meteetsee, but he went over the Divide and killed that old fellow that had once chased him out of the Warhouse Valley. And, more than that, he held what he had won, for he broke up a camp of tenderfeet that were looking for a ranch location on the Middle Meteetsee; he stampeded their horses, and made general smash of the camp. And so all the animals, including man, came to know that the whole range from Frank's Peak to the Shoshone spurs was the proper domain of a king well able to defend it, and the name of that king was Meteetsee Wahb.

Any creature whose strength puts him beyond danger of open attack is apt to lose in cunning. Yet Wahb never forgot his early experience with the traps. He made it a rule never to go near that smell of man and iron, and that was the reason that he never again was caught.

So he led his lonely life and slouched around on the mountains, throwing boulders about like pebbles, and huge trunks like matchwood, as he sought for his daily food. And every beast of hill and plain soon came to know and fly in fear of Wahb, the one time hunted, persecuted Cub. And more than one Black bear paid with his life for the ill-deed of that other, long ago. And many a cranky Bobcat flying before him took to a tree, and if that tree were dead and dry, Wahb heaved it down, and tree and Cat alike were dashed to bits. Even the proud-necked Stallion, leader of the mustang band, thought well for once to yield the road. The great, grey Timber wolves, and the Mountain Lions too, left their new kill and sneaked in sullen fear aside when Wahb appeared. And if, as he hulked across the sage-covered river-flat sending the scared Antelope skimming like birds before him, he was faced perchance, by some burly Range-bull, too young to be wise and too big to be afraid, Wahb smashed his skull with one blow of that giant paw, and served him as the Range- cow would have served himself long years ago.

The All-mother never fails to offer to her own, twin cups, one gall, and one of balm. Little or much they may drink, but equally of each. The mountain that is easy to descend must soon be climbed again. The grinding hardship of Wahb's early days, had built his mighty frame. All usual pleasures of a grizzly's life had been denied him but power bestowed in more than double share. So he lived on year after year, unsoftened by mate or companion, sullen, fearing nothing, ready to fight, but asking only to be let alone--quite alone. He had but one keen pleasure in his sombre life--the lasting glory in his matchless strength--the small but never failing thrill of joy as the foe fell crushed and limp, or the riven boulders grit and heaved when he turned on them the measure of his wondrous force.

IV.

Everything has a smell of its own for those that have noses to smell. Wahb had been learning smells all his life, and knew the meaning of most of those in the mountains. It was as though each and every thing had a voice of its own for him; and yet it was far better than a voice, for every one knows that a good nose is better than eyes and ears together. And each of these myriads of voices kept on crying, "Here and such am I."

The juniper-berries, the rosehips, the strawberries, each had a soft, sweet little voice, calling, "Here we are--Berries, Berries."

The great pine woods had a loud, far-reaching voice, "Here are we, the Pine-trees," but when he got right up to them Wahb could hear the low, sweet call of the nuts, "Here are we, the nuts."

And the quamash beds in May sang a perfect chorus when the wind was right: "Quamash beds, Quamash beds."

And when he got among them he made out each single voice.

Each root had its own little piece to say to his nose: "Here am I, a big Quamash, rich and ripe," or a tiny, sharp voice, "Here am I, a good-for-nothing, stringy little root."

And the broad, rich russulas in the autumn called aloud, "I am a fat, wholesome Mushroom," and the deadly amanita cried, "I am an Amanita. Let me alone, or you'll be a sick Bear." And the fairy harebell of the canyon-banks sang a song too, as fine as its threadlike stem, and as soft as its dainty blue; but the warden of the smells had learned to report it not, for this, and a million other such, were of no interest to Wahb.

So every living thing that moved, and every flower that grew, and every rock and stone and shape on earth told out its tale and sang its little story to his nose. Day or night, fog or bright, that great, moist nose told him most of the things he needed to know, or passed unnoticed those of no concern, and he depended on it more and more. If his eyes and ears together reported so and so, he would not even then believe it until his nose said, "Yes; that is right."

But this is something that man cannot understand, for he has sold the birthright of his nose for the privilege of living in towns.

While hundreds of smells were agreeable to Wahb, thousands were indifferent to him, a good many were unpleasant, and some actually put him in a rage.

He had often noticed that if a west wind were blowing when he was at the head of the Piney Canyon there was an odd, new scent. Some days he did not mind, it, and some days it disgusted him; but he never followed it up. On other days a north wind from the high Divide brought a most awful smell, something unlike any other, a smell that he wanted only to get away from.

Wahb was getting well past his youth now, and he began to have pains in the hind leg that had been wounded so often. After a cold night or a long time of wet weather he could scarcely use that leg, and one day, while thus crippled, the west wind came down the canyon with an odd message to his nose. Wahb could not clearly read the message, but it seemed to say, 'Come,' and something within him said, 'Go.' The smell of food will draw a hungry creature and disgust a gorged one. We do not know why, and all that any one can learn is that the desire springs from a need of the body. So Wahb felt drawn by what had long disgusted him, and he slouched up the mountain path, grumbling to himself and slapping savagely back at branches that chanced to switch his face.

The odd odor grew very strong; it led him where he had never been before--up a bank of whitish sand to a bench of the same color, where there was unhealthy-looking water running down, and a kind of fog coming out of a hole. Wahb threw up his nose suspiciously--such a peculiar smell! He climbed the bench.

A snake wriggled across the sand in front. Wahb crushed it with a blow that made the near trees shiver and sent a balanced boulder toppling down, and he growled a growl that rumbled up the valley like distant thunder. Then he came to the foggy hole. It was full of water that moved gently and steamed. Wahb put in his foot, and found it was quite warm and that it felt pleasantly on his skin. He put in both feet, and little by little went in farther, causing the pool to overflow on all sides, till he was lying at full length in the warm, almost hot, sulphur-spring, and sweltering in the greenish water, while the wind drifted the steam about overhead.

There are plenty of these sulphur-springs in the Rockies, but this chanced to be the only one on Wahb's range. He lay in it for over an hour; then, feeling that he had had enough, he heaved his huge bulk up on the bank, and realized that he was feeling remarkably well and supple. The stiffness of his hind leg was gone.

He shook the water from his shaggy coat. A broad ledge in full sun-heat invited him to stretch himself out and dry. But first he reared against the nearest tree and left a mark that none could mistake. True, there were plenty of signs of other animals using the sulphur-bath for their ills; but what of it? Thenceforth that tree bore this inscription, in a language of mud, hair, and smell, that every mountain creature could read:

My bath. Keep away!

(Signed) WAHB.

Wahb lay on his belly till his back was dry, then turned on his broad back and squirmed about in a ponderous way till the broiling sun had wholly dried him. He realized that he was really feeling very well now. He did not say to himself, "I am troubled with that unpleasant disease called rheumatism, and sulphur-bath treatment is the thing to cure it." But what he did know was, "I have dreadful pains; I feel better when I am in this stinking pool." So thenceforth he came back whenever the pains began again, and each time he was cured.

PART III.

THE WANING

I.

Years went by. Wahb grew no bigger,--there was no need for that,--but he got whiter, crosser, and more dangerous. He really had an enormous range now. Each spring, after the winter storms had removed his notice-boards, he went around and renewed them. It was natural to do so, for, first of all, the scarcity of food compelled him to travel all over the range. There were lots of clay wallows at that season, and the itching of his skin, as the winter coat began to shed, made the dressing of cool, wet clay very pleasant, and the exquisite pain of a good scratching was one of the finest pleasures he knew. So, whatever his motive, the result was the same: the signs were renewed each spring.

At length the Palette Ranch outfit appeared on the Lower Piney, and the men got acquainted with the 'ugly old fellow.' The Cowpunchers, when they saw him, decided they 'had n't lost any Bears and they had better keep out of his way and let him mind his business.'

They did not often see him, although his tracks and sign-boards were everywhere. But the owner of this outfit, a born hunter, took a keen interest in Wahb. He learned something of the old Bear's history from Colonel Pickett, and found out for himself more than the colonel ever knew.

He learned that Wahb ranged as far south as the Upper Wiggins Fork and north to the Stinking Water, and from the Meteetsee to the Shoshones.

He found that Wahb knew more about Bear-traps than most trappers do; that he either passed them by or tore open the other end of the bait-pen and dragged out the bait without going near the trap, and by accident or design Wahb sometimes sprang the trap with one of the logs that formed the pen. This ranch-owner found also that Wahb disappeared from his range each year during the heat of the summer, as completely as he did each winter during his sleep.

II.

Many years ago a wise government set aside the head waters of the Yellowstone to be a sanctuary of wild life forever. In the limits of this great Wonderland the ideal of the Royal Singer was to be realized, and none were to harm or make afraid. No violence was to be offered to any bird or beast, no ax was to be carried into its primitive forests, and the streams were to flow on forever unpolluted by mill or mine. All things were to bear witness that such as this was the West before the white man came.

The wild animals quickly found out all this. They soon learned the boundaries of this unfenced Park, and, as every one knows, they show a different nature within its sacred limits. They no longer shun the face of man, they neither fear nor attack him, and they are even more tolerant of one another in this land of refuge.

Peace and plenty are the sum of earthly good; so, finding them here, the wild creatures crowd into the Park from the surrounding country in numbers not elsewhere to be seen.

The Bears are especially numerous about the Fountain Hotel. In the woods, a quarter of a mile away, is a smooth open place where the steward of the hotel has all the broken and waste food put out daily for the Bears, and the man whose work it is has become the Steward of the Bears' Banquet. Each day it is spread, and each year there are more Bears to partake of it. It is a common thing now to see a dozen Bears feasting there at one time. They are of all kinds--Black, Brown, Cinnamon, Grizzly, Silvertip, Roach-backs, big and small, families and rangers, from all parts of the vast surrounding country. All seem to realize that in the Park no violence is allowed, and the most ferocious of them have here put on a new behavior. Although scores of Bears roam about this choice resort, and sometimes quarrel among themselves, not one of them has ever yet harmed a man.

Year after year they have come and gone. The passing travelers see them. The men of the hotel know many of them well. They know that they show up each summer during the short season when the hotel is in use, and that they disappear again, no man knowing whence they come or whither they go.

One day the owner of the Palette Ranch came through the Park. During his stay at the Fountain Hotel, he went to the Bear banquet-hall at high meal-tide. There were several Blackbears feasting, but they made way for a huge Silvertip Grizzly that came about sundown.

"That," said the man who was acting as guide, "is the biggest Grizzly in the Park; but he is a peaceable sort, or Lud knows what'd happen."

"That!" said the ranchman, in astonishment, as the Grizzly came hulking nearer, and loomed up like a load of hay among the piney pillars of the Banquet Hall. "That! It that is not Meteetsee Wahb, I never saw a Bear in my life! Why, that is the worst Grizzly that ever rolled a log in the Big Horn Basin." "It ain't possible," said the other, "for he's here every summer, July and August, an' I reckon he don't live so far away."

"Well, that settles it," said the ranchman; "July and August is just the time we miss him on the range; and you can see for yourself that he is a little lame behind and has lost a claw of his left front foot. Now I know where he puts in his summers; but I did not suppose that the old reprobate would know enough to behave himself away from home."

The big Grizzly became very well known during the successive hotel seasons. Once only did he really behave ill, and that was the first season he appeared, before he fully knew the ways of the Park.

He wandered over to the hotel, one day, and in at the front door. In the hall he reared up his eight feet of stature as the guests fled in terror; then he went into the clerk's office. The man said: "All right; if you need this office more than I do, you can have it," and leaping over the counter, locked himself in the telegraph-office, to wire the superintendent of the Park: "Old Grizzly in the office now, seems to want to run hotel; may we shoot?"

The reply came: "No shooting allowed in Park; use the hose." Which they did, and, wholly taken by surprise, the Bear leaped over the counter too, and ambled out the back way, with a heavy thud-thudding of his feet, and a rattling of his claws on the floor. He passed through the kitchen as he went, and, picking up a quarter of beef, took it along.

This was the only time he was known to do ill, though on one occasion he was led into a breach of the peace by another Bear. This was a large she-Blackbear and a noted mischief-maker. She had a wretched, sickly cub that she was very proud of--so proud that she went out of her way to seek trouble on his behalf. And he, like all spoiled children, was the cause of much bad feeling. She was so big and fierce that she could bully all the other Black bears, but when she tried to drive off old Wahb she received a pat from his paw that sent her tumbling like a football. He followed her up, and would have killed her, for she had broken the peace of the Park, but she escaped by climbing a tree, from the top of which her miserable little cub was apprehensively squealing at the pitch of his voice. So the affair was ended; in future the Blackbear kept out of Wahb's way, and he won the reputation of being a peaceable, well-behaved Bear. Most persons believed that he came from some remote mountains where were neither guns nor traps to make him sullen and revengeful.

III.

Every one knows that a Bitter-root Grizzly is a bad Bear. The Bitter-root Range is the roughest part of the mountains. The ground is everywhere cut up with deep ravines and overgrown with dense and tangled underbrush.

It is an impossible country for horses, and difficult for gunners, and there is any amount of good Bear-pasture. So there are plenty of Bears and plenty of trappers.

The Roachbacks, as the Bitter-root Grizzlies are called, are a cunning and desperate race. An old Roachback knows more about traps than half a dozen ordinary trappers; he knows more about plants and roots than a whole college of botanists. He can tell to a certainty just when and where to find each kind of grub and worm, and he knows by a whiff whether the hunter on his trail a mile away is working with guns, poison, dogs, traps, or all of them together. And he has one general rule, which is an endless puzzle to the hunter: 'Whatever you decide to do, do it quickly and follow it right up.' So when a trapper and a Roachback meet, the Bear at once makes up his mind to run away as hard as he can, or to rush at the man and fight to a finish.

The Grizzlies of the Bad Lands did not do this: they used to stand on their dignity and growl like a thunder-storm, and so gave the hunters a chance to play their deadly lightning; and lightning is worse than thunder any day. Men can get used to growls that rumble along the ground and up one's legs to the little house where one's courage lives; but Bears cannot get used to 45-90 soft-nosed bullets, and that is why the Grizzlies of the Bad Lands were all killed off.

So the hunters have learned that they never know what a Roachback will do; but they do know that he is going to be quick about it.

Altogether these Bitter-root Grizzlies have solved very well the problem of life, in spite of white men, and are therefore increasing in their own wild mountains.

Of course a range will hold only so many Bears, and the increase is crowded out; so that when that slim young Bald-faced Roachback found he could not hold the range he wanted, he went out perforce to seek his fortune in the world.

He was not a big Bear, or he would not have been crowded out; but he had been trained in a good school, so that he was cunning enough to get on very well elsewhere. How he wandered down to the Salmon River Mountains and did not like them; how he traveled till he got among the barb-wire fences of the Snake Plains and of course could not stay there; how a mere chance turned him from going eastward to the Park, where he might have rested; how he made for the Snake River Mountains and found more hunters than berries; how he crossed into the Tetons and looked down with disgust on the teeming man colony of Jackson's Hole, does not belong to this history of Wahb. But when Baldy Roachback crossed the Gros Ventre Range and over the Wind River Divide to the head of the Graybull, he does come into the story, just as he did into the country and the life of the Meteetsee Grizzly.

The Roachback had not found a man-sign since he left Jackson's Hole, and here he was in a land of plenty of food. He feasted on all the delicacies of the season, and enjoyed the easy, brushless country till he came on one of Wahb's sign-posts.

"Trespassers beware!" it said in the plainest manner. The Roachback reared up against it.

"Thunder! what a Bear!" The nose-mark was a head and neck above Baldy's highest reach. Now, a simple Bear would have gone quietly away after this discovery; but Baldy felt that the mountains owed him a living, and here was a good one if he could keep out of the way of the big fellow. He nosed about the place, kept a sharp lookout for the present owner, and went on feeding wherever he ran across a good thing.

A step or two from this ominous tree was an old pine stump. In the Bitter-roots there are often mice-nests under such stumps, and Baldy jerked it over to see. There was nothing. The stump rolled over against the sign-post. Baldy had not yet made up his mind about it; but a new notion came into his cunning brain. He turned his head on this side, then on that. He looked at the stump, then at the sign, with his little pig-like eyes. Then he deliberately stood up on the pine root, with his back to the tree, and put his mark away up, a head at least above that of Wahb. He rubbed his back long and hard, and he sought some mud to smear his head and shoulders, then came back and made the mark so big, so strong, and so high, and emphasized it with such claw-gashes in the bark, that it could be read only in one way--a challenge to the present claimant from some monstrous invader, who was ready, nay anxious, to fight to a finish for this desirable range.

Maybe it was accident and maybe design, but when the Roach-back jumped from the root it rolled to one side. Baldy went on down the ca 駉 n, keeping the keenest lookout for his enemy.

It was not long before Wahb found the trail of the interloper, and all the ferocity of his outside-the-Park nature was aroused.

He followed the trail for miles on more than one occasion. But the small Bear was quick-footed as well as quick-witted, and never showed himself. He made a point, however, of calling at each sign-post, and if there was any means of cheating, so that his mark might be put higher, he did it with a vim, and left a big, showy record. But if there was no chance for any but a fair register, he would not go near the tree, but looked for a fresh tree near by with some log or side-ledge to reach from.

Thus Wahb soon found the interloper's marks towering far above his own--a monstrous Bear evidently, that even he could not be sure of mastering. But Wahb was no coward. He was ready to fight to a finish any one that might come; and he hunted the range for that invader. Day after day Wahb sought for him and held himself ready to fight. He found his trail daily, and more and more often he found that towering record far above his own. He often smelled him on the wind; but he never saw him, for the old Grizzly's eyes had grown very dim of late years; things but a little way off were blurs to him. The continual menace could not but fill Wahb with uneasiness, for he was not young now, and his teeth and claws were worn and blunted. He was more than ever troubled with pains in his old wounds, and though he could have risen on the spur of the moment to fight any number of Grizzlies of any size, still the continual apprehension, the knowledge that he must hold himself ready at any moment to fight this young monster, weighed on his spirits and began to tell on his general health.

IV.

The Roachback's life was one of continual vigilance, always ready to run, doubling and shifting to avoid the encounter that must mean instant death to him. Many a time from some hiding-place he watched the great Bear, and trembled lest the wind should betray him. Several times his very impudence saved him, and more than once he was nearly cornered in a box-canyon. Once he escaped only by climbing up a long crack in a cliff, which Wahb's huge frame could not have entered. But still, in a mad persistence, he kept on marking the trees farther into the range.

At last he scented and followed up the sulphur-bath. He did not understand it at all. It had no appeal to him, but hereabouts were the tracks of the owner. In a spirit of mischief the Roachback scratched dirt into the spring, and then seeing the rubbing-tree, he stood sidewise on the rocky ledge, and was thus able to put his mark fully five feet above that of Wahb. Then he nervously jumped down, and was running about, defiling the bath and keeping a sharp lookout, when he heard a noise in the woods below. Instantly he was all alert. The sound drew near, then the wind brought the sure proof, and the Roachback, in terror, turned and fled into the woods.

It was Wahb. He had been failing in health of late; his old pains were on him again, and, as well as his hind leg, had seized his right shoulder, where were still lodged two rifle-balls. He was feeling very ill, and crippled with pain. He came up the familiar bank at a jerky limp, and there caught the odor of the foe; then he saw the track in the mud--his eyes said the track of a small Bear, but his eyes were dim now, and his nose, his unerring nose, said, "This is the track of the huge invader." Then he noticed the tree with his sign on it, and there beyond doubt was the stranger's mark far above his own. His eyes and nose were agreed on this; and more, they told him that the foe was close at hand, might at any moment come.

Wahb was feeling ill and weak with pain. He was in no mood for a desperate fight. A battle against such odds would be madness now. So, without taking the treatment, he turned and swung along the bench away from the direction taken by the stranger--the first time since his cubhood that he had declined to fight.

That was a turning-point in Wahb's life. If he had followed up the stranger he would have found the miserable little craven trembling, cowering, in an agony of terror, behind a log in a natural trap, a walled-in glade only fifty yards away, and would surely have crushed him. Had he even taken the bath, his strength and courage would have been renewed, and if not, then at least in time he would have met his foe, and his after life would have been different. But he had turned. This was the fork in the trail, but he had no means of knowing it.

He limped along, skirting the lower spurs of the Shoshones, and soon came on that horrid smell that he had known for years, but never followed up or understood. It was right in his road, and he traced it to a small, barren ravine that was strewn over with skeletons and dark objects, and Wahb, as he passed, smelled a smell of many different animals, and knew by its quality that they were lying dead in this treeless, grassless hollow. For there was a cleft in the rocks at the upper end, whence poured a deadly gas; invisible but heavy, it filled the little gulch like a brimming poison bowl, and at the lower end there was a steady overflow. But Wahb knew only that the air that poured from it as he passed made him dizzy and sleepy, and repelled him, so that he got quickly away from it and was glad once more to breathe the piny wind. Once Wahb decided to retreat, it was all too easy to do so next time; and the result worked double disaster. For, since the big stranger was allowed possession of the sulphur-spring, Wahb felt that he would rather not go there. Sometimes when he came across the traces of his foe, a spurt of his old courage would come back. He would rumble that thunder-growl as of old, and go painfully lumbering along the trail to settle the thing right then and there. But he never overtook the mysterious giant, and his rheumatism, growing worse now that he was barred from the cure, soon made him daily less capable of either running or fighting.

Sometimes Wahb would sense his foe's approach when he was in a bad place for fighting, and, without really running, he would yield to a wish to be on a better footing, where he would have a fair chance. This better footing never led him nearer the enemy, for it is well known that the one awaiting has the advantage.

Some days Wahb felt so ill that it would have been madness to have staked everything on a fight, and when he felt well or a little better, the stranger seemed to keep away.

Wahb soon found that the stranger's track was most often on the Warhouse and the west slope of the Piney, the very best feeding-grounds. To avoid these when he did not feel equal to fighting was only natural, and as he was always in more or less pain now, it amounted to abandoning to the stranger the best part of the range.

Weeks went by. Wahb had meant to go back to his bath, but he never did. His pains grew worse; he was now crippled in his right shoulder as well as in his hind leg.

The long strain of waiting for the fight begot anxiety, that grew to be apprehension, which, with the sapping of his strength, was breaking down his courage, as it always must when courage is founded on muscular force. His daily care now was not to meet and fight the invader, but to avoid him till he felt better.

Thus that first little retreat grew into one long retreat. Wahb had to go farther and farther down the Piney to avoid an encounter. He was daily worse fed, and as the weeks went by was daily less able to crush a foe.

He was living and hiding at last on the Lower Piney--the very place where once his Mother had brought him with his little brothers. The life he led now was much like the one he had led after that dark day. Perhaps for the same reason. If he had had a family of his own all might have been different. As he limped along one morning, seeking among the barren aspen groves for a few roots, or the wormy partridge-berries that were too poor to interest the Squirrel and the Grouse, he heard a stone rattle down the western slope into the woods, and, a little later, on the wind was borne the dreaded taint. He waded through the ice-cold Piney,--once he would have leaped it,--and the chill water sent through and up each great hairy limb keen pains that seemed to reach his very life. He was retreating again--which way? There seemed but one way now--toward the new ranch-house.

But there were signs of stir about it long before he was near enough to be seen. His nose, his trustiest friend, said, "Turn, turn and seek the hills," and turn he did even at the risk of meeting there the dreadful foe. He limped painfully along the north bank of the Piney, keeping in the hollows and among the trees. He tried to climb a cliff that of old he had often bounded up at full speed. When half-way up his footing gave way, and down he rolled to the bottom. A long way round was now the only road, for onward he must go--on--on. But where? There seemed no choice now but to abandon the whole range to the terrible stranger.

And feeling, as far as a Bear can feel, that he is fallen, defeated, dethroned at last, that he is driven from his ancient range by a Bear too strong for him to face, he turned up the west fork, and the lot was drawn. The strength and speed were gone from his once mighty limbs; he took three times as long as he once would to mount each well-known ridge, and as he went he glanced backward from time to time to know if he were pursued. Away up the head of the little branch were the Shoshones, bleak, forbidding; no enemies were there, and the Park was beyond it all--on, on he must go. But as he climbed with shaky limbs, and short uncertain steps, the west wind brought the odor of Death Gulch, that fearful little valley where everything was dead, where the very air was deadly. It used to disgust him and drive him away, but now Wahb felt that it had a message for him; he was drawn by it. It was in his line of flight, and he hobbled slowly toward the place. He went nearer, nearer, until he stood upon the entering ledge. A Vulture that had descended to feed on one of the victims was slowly going to sleep on the untouched carcass. Wahb swung his great grizzled muzzle and his long white beard in the wind. The odor that he once had hated was attractive now. There was a strange biting quality in the air. His body craved it. For it seemed to numb his pain and it promised sleep, as it did that day when first he saw the place.

Far below him, to the right and to the left and on and on as far as the eye could reach, was the great kingdom that once had been his; where he had lived for years in the glory of his strength; where none had dared to meet him face to face. The whole earth could show no view more beautiful. But Wahb had no thought of its beauty; he only knew that it was a good land to live in; that it had been his, but that now it was gone, for his strength was gone, and he was flying to seek a place where he could rest and be at peace.

Away over the Shoshones, indeed, was the road to the Park, but it was far, far away, with a doubtful end to the long, doubtful journey. But why so far? Here in this little gulch was all he sought; here were peace and painless sleep. He knew it; for his nose, his never-erring nose, said, "Here! here now!"

He paused a moment at the gate, and as he stood the wind-borne fumes began their subtle work. Five were the faithful wardens of his life, and the best and trustiest of them all flung open wide the door he long had kept. A moment still Wahb stood in doubt. His lifelong guide was silent now, had given up his post. But another sense he felt within. The Angel of the Wild Things was standing there, beckoning, in the little vale. Wahb did not understand. He had no eyes to see the tear in the Angel's eyes, nor the pitying smile that was surely on his lips. He could not even see the Angel. But he felt him beckoning, beckoning. A rush of his ancient courage surged in the Grizzly's rugged breast. He turned aside into the little gulch. The deadly vapors entered in, filled his huge chest and tingled in his vast, heroic limbs as he calmly lay down on the rocky, herbless floor and as gently went to sleep, as he did that day in his Mother's arms by the Graybull, long ago.

THE END

The Trail of the Sandhill Stag

by Ernest Seton-Thompson

I

It was a burning hot day. Yan was wandering in pursuit of birds among the endless groves and glades of the Sandhill wilderness about Carberry. The water in the numerous marshy ponds was warm with the sun heat, so Yan cut across to the trail spring, the only place in the country where he might find a cooling drink. As he stooped beside it his eye fell on a small hoof-mark in the mud, a sharp and elegant track.

He had never seen one like it before, but it gave him a thrill, for he knew at once it was the track of a wild deer.

"There are no deer in those hills now," the settlers told Yan. Yet when the first snow came that autumn he, remembering the hoof-mark in the mud, quietly took down his rifle and said to himself, "I am going into the hills every day till I bring out a deer." Yan was a tall, raw lad in the last of his teens. He was no hunter yet, but he was a tireless runner, and filled with unflagging zeal. Away to the hills he went on his quest day after day, and many a score of long white miles he coursed, and night after night he returned to the shanty without seeing even a track. But the longest chase will end. On a far, hard trip in the southern hills he came at last on the trail of a deer--dim and stale, but still a deer-trail--and again he felt a thrill as the thought came, "At the other end of that line of dimples in the snow is the creature that made them; each one is fresher than the last, and it is only a question of time for me to come up with their maker."

At first Yan could not tell by the dim track which way the animal had gone. But he soon found that the mark was a little sharper at one end, and rightly guessed that that was the toe; also he noticed that the spaces shortened in going up hill, and at last a clear imprint in a sandy place ended all doubt. Away he went with a new fire in his blood, and an odd prickling in his hair; away on a long, hard follow through interminable woods and hills, with the trail growing fresher as he flew. All day he followed, and toward night it turned and led him homeward. On it went, soon over familiar ground, back to the sawmill, then over Mitchell's Plain, and at last into the thick poplar woods near by, where Yan left it when it was too dark to follow. He was only seven miles from home, and this he easily trotted in an hour.

In the morning he was back to take it up, but instead of an old track, there were now so many fresh ones, crossing and winding, that he could not follow at all. So he prowled along haphazard, until he found two tracks so new that he could easily trail them as before, and he eagerly gave chase. As he sneaked along watching the tracks at his feet instead of the woods ahead, he was startled by two big-eared, grayish animals springing from a little glade into which he had stumbled. They trotted to a bank fifty yards away and then turned to gaze at him.

How they did seem to look with their great ears! How they spellbound him by the soft gaze that he felt rather than saw! He knew what they were. Had he not for weeks been holding ready, preparing and hungering for this very sight! And yet how useless were his preparations; how wholly all his preconcepts were swept away, and a wonder-stricken

"Oh-h-h!" went softly from his throat.

As he stood and gazed, they turned their heads away, though they still seemed to look at him with their great ears, and trotting a few steps to a smoother place, began to bound up and down in a sort of play. They seemed to have forgotten him, and it was bewildering to see the wonderful effortless way in which, by a tiny toe-touch, they would rise six or eight feet in air. Yan stood fascinated by the strange play of the light-limbed, gray-furred creatures. There was no haste or alarm in their movements; he would watch them until they began to run away--till they should take fright and begin the labored straining, the vast athletic bounds, he had heard of.

And it was only on noting that they were rapidly fading into the distance that he realized that now they were running away, already were flying for safety.

Higher and higher they rose each time; gracefully their bodies swayed inward as they curved along some bold ridge, or for a long space the buff-white scutcheons that they bore behind them seemed hanging in the air while these wingless birds were really sailing over some deep gully.

Yan stood intensely gazing until they were out of sight, and it never once occurred to him to shoot.

When they were gone he went to the place where they had begun their play. Here was one track; where was the next? He looked all around and was surprised to see a blank for fifteen feet; and then another blank, and on farther, another: then the blanks increased to eighteen feet, then to twenty, then to twenty-five and sometimes thirty feet. Each of these playful, effortless bounds covered a space of eighteen to thirty feet.

Gods above! They do not run at all, they fly; and once in a while come down again to tap the hill-tops with their dainty hoofs.

* * * * *

"I'm glad they got away," said Yan. "They've shown me something to-day that never man saw before. I know that no one else has ever seen it, or he would have told of it."

II

Yet when the morning came the old wolfish instinct was back in his heart. "I must away to the hills," he said, "take up the trail, and be a beast of the chase once more; my wits against their wits; my strength against their strength; and against their speed, my gun."

Oh! those glorious hills--an endless rolling stretch of sandy dunes, with lakes and woods and grassy lawns between. Life--life on every side, and life within, for Yan was young and strong and joyed in powers complete. "These are the best days of my life," he said, "these are my golden days." He thought it then, and oh, how well he came to know it in the after years!

All day at a long wolf-lope he would go and send the white hare and the partridge flying from his path, and swing along and scan the ground for sign and the telltale inscript in the snow, the oldest of all writing, more thrillful of interest by far than the finest glyph or scarab that ever Egypt gave to modern day.

But the driving snow was the wild deer's friend, as the driven snow was his foe, and down it came that day and wiped out every trace.

The next day and the next still found Yan careering in the hills, but never a track or sign did he see. And the weeks went by, and many a rolling mile he ran, and many a bitter day and freezing night he passed in the snow-clad hills, sometimes on a deer-trail but more often without; sometimes in the barren hills, and sometimes led by woodmen's talk to far-off sheltering woods, and once or twice he saw indeed the buff-white bannerets go floating up the hills. Sometimes reports came of a great buck that frequented the timber-lands near the sawmill, and more than once Yan found his trail, but never got a glimpse of him; and the few deer there were now grew so wild with long pursuit that he had no further chances to shoot, and the hunting season passed in one long train of failures.

Bright, unsad failures they. He seemed indeed to come back empty-handed, but he really came home laden with the best spoils of the chase, and he knew it more and more, as time went on, till every day, at last, on the clear unending trail, was a glad triumphant march.

III

The year went by. Another season came, and Yan felt in his heart the hunter fret once more. Even had he not, the talk he heard would have set him all afire.

It told of a mighty buck that now lived in the hills--the Sandhill Stag they called him. It told of his size, his speed, and the crowning glory that he bore on his brow, a marvellous growth like sculptured bronze with gleaming ivory points.

So when the first tracking snow came, Yan set out with some comrades who had caught a faint reflected glow of his ardor. They drove in a sleigh to the Spruce Hill, then scattered to meet again at sunset. The woods about abounded in hares and grouse, and the powder burned all around. But no deer-track was to be found, so Yan quietly left the woods and set off alone for Kennedy's Plain, where last this wonderful buck had been seen.

After a few miles he came on a great deer-track, so large and sharp and broken by such mighty bounds that he knew it at once for the trail of the Sandhill Stag.

With a sudden rush of strength to his limbs he led away like a wolf on the trail. And down his spine and in his hair he felt as before, and yet as never before, the strange prickling that he knew was the same as makes the wolf's mane bristle when he hunts. He followed till night was near and he must needs turn, for the Spruce Hill was many miles away.

He knew that it would be long after sunset before he could get there, and he scarcely expected that his comrades would wait for him, but he did not care; he gloried in the independence of his strength, for his legs were like iron and his wind was like a hound's. Ten miles were no more to him than a mile to another man, for he could run all day and come home fresh, and always when alone in the lone hills he felt within so glad a gush of wild exhilaration that his joy was full.

So when his friends, feeling sure that he could take care of himself, drove home and left him, he was glad to be left. They seemed rather to pity him for imposing on himself such long, toilsome tramps. They had no realization of what he found in those wind-swept hills. They never once thought what they and all their friends and every man that ever lived has striven for and offered his body, his brain, his freedom, and his life to buy; what they were vainly wearing out their lives in fearful, hopeless drudgery to gain, that boy was daily finding in those hills. The bitter, biting, blizzard wind was without, but the fire of health and youth was within; and at every stride in his daily march, it was happiness he found, and he knew it. And he smiled such a gentle smile when he thought of those driven home in the sleigh shivering and miserable, yet pitying him.

Oh, what a glorious sunset he saw that day on Kennedy's Plain, with the snow dyed red and the poplar woods aglow in pink and gold! What a glorious tramp through the darkening woods as the shadows fell and the yellow moon came up!

"These are the best days of my life," he sang. "These are my golden days!"

And as he neared the great Spruce Hill, Yan yelled a long hurrah! "In case they are still there," he told himself, but really for very joy of feeling all alive.

As he listened for the improbable response, he heard a faint howling of wolves away over Kennedy's Plain. He mimicked their cry and quickly got response, and noticed that they were gathering together, doubtless hunting something, for now it was their hunting-cry. Nearer and nearer it came, and his howls brought ready answers from the gloomy echoing woods, when suddenly it flashed upon him: "It's my trail you are on. You are hunting me."

The road now led across a little open plain. It would have been madness to climb a tree in such a fearful frost, so he went out to the middle of the open place and sat down in the moonlit snow--a glittering rifle in his hands, a row of shining brass pegs in his belt, and a strange, new feeling in his heart. On came the chorus, a deep, melodious howling, on to the very edge of the woods, and there the note changed. Then there was silence. They must have seen him sitting there, for the light was like day, but they went around in the edge of the woods. A stick snapped to the right and a low 'Woof' came from the left. Then all was still. Yan felt them sneaking around, felt them watching him from the cover, and strained his eyes in vain to see some form that he might shoot. But they were wise, and he was wise, for had he run he would soon have seen them closing in on him. They must have been but few, for after their council of war they decided he was better let alone, and he never saw them at all. For twenty minutes he waited, but hearing no more of them, arose and went homeward. And as he tramped he thought, "Now I know how a deer feels when the grind of a moccasined foot or the click of a lock is heard in the trail behind him."

In the days that followed he learned those Sandhills well, for many a frosty day and bitter night he spent in them. He learned to follow fast the faintest trail of deer. He learned just why that trail went never past a tamarack-tree, and why it pawed the snow at every oak, and why the buck's is plainest and the fawn's down wind. He learned just what the club-rush has to say, when its tussocks break the snow. He came to know how the musk-rat lives beneath the ice, and why the mink slides down a hill, and what the ice says when it screams at night. The squirrels taught him how best a fir-cone can be stripped and which of toadstools one might eat. The partridge, why it dives beneath the snow, and the fox, just why he sets his feet so straight, and why he wears so huge a tail.

He learned the ponds, the woods, the hills, and a hundred secrets of the trail, but--he got no deer.

And though many a score of crooked frosty miles he coursed, and sometimes had a track to lead and sometimes none, he still went on, like Galahad when the Grail was just before him. For more than once, the guide that led was the trail of the Sandhill Stag.

IV

The hunt was nearly over, for the season's end was nigh. The moose-birds had picked the last of the saskatoons, all the spruce-cones were scaled, and the hunger-moon was at hand. But a hopeful chickadee sang 'See soon' as Yan set off one frosty day for the great Spruce Woods. On the road he overtook a woodcutter, who told him that at such a place he had seen two deer last night, a doe and a monstrous stag with "a rocking-chair on his head."

Straight to the very place went Yan, and found the tracks--one like those he had seen in the mud long ago, another a large unmistakable print, the mark of the Sandhill Stag.

How the wild beast in his heart did ramp--he wanted to howl like a wolf on a hot scent; and away they went through woods and hills, the trail and Yan and the inner wolf.

All day he followed and, grown crafty himself, remarked each sign, and rejoiced to find that nowhere had the deer been bounding. And when the sun was low the sign was warm, so laying aside unneeded things, Yan crawled along like a snake on the track of a hare. All day the animals had zigzagged as they fed; their drink was snow, and now at length away across a lawn in a bank of brush Yan spied a something flash. A bird perhaps; he lay still and watched. Then gray among the gray brush, he made out a great log, and from one end of it rose two gnarled oaken boughs. Again the flash--the move of a restless ear, then the oak boughs moved and Yan trembled, for he knew that the log in the brush was the form of the Sandhill Stag. So grand, so charged with life. He seemed a precious, sacred thing--a king, fur-robed and duly crowned. To think of shooting now as he lay unconscious, resting, seemed an awful crime. But Yan for weeks and months had pined for this. His chance had come, and shoot he must. The long, long strain grew tighter yet--grew taut--broke down, as up the rifle went. But the wretched thing kept wabbling and pointing all about the little glade. His breath came hot and fast and choking--so much, so very much, so clearly all, hung on a single touch. He laid the rifle down, revulsed--and trembled in the snow. But he soon regained the mastery, his hand was steady now, the sights in line--'twas but a deer out yonder. But at that moment the Stag turned full Yan's way, with those regardful eyes and ears, and nostrils too, and gazed.

"Darest thou slay me?" said an uncrowned, unarmed king once, as his eyes fell on the assassin's knife, and in that clear, calm gaze the murderer quailed and cowed.

So trembled Yan; but he knew it was only stag-fever, and he despised it then as he came in time to honor it; and the beast that dwelt within him fired the gun.

The ball splashed short. The buck sprang up and the doe appeared. Another shot; then, as they fled, another and another. But away the deer went, lightly drifting across the low round hills.

V

He followed their trail for some time, but gnashed his teeth to find no sign of blood, and he burned with a raging animal sense that was neither love nor hate. Within a mile there was a new sign that joined on and filled him with another rage and shed light on many a bloody page of frontier history--a moccasin-track, a straight-set, broad-toed, moosehide track, the track of a Cree brave. He followed in savage humor, and as he careered up a slope a tall form rose from a log, raising one hand in peaceable gesture. Although Yan was behind, the Indian had seen him first.

"Who are you?" said Yan, roughly.

"Chaska."

"What are you doing in my country?"

"It was my country first," he replied gravely.

"Those are my deer," Yan said, and thought.

"No man owns wild deer till he kills them," said Chaska.

"You better keep off any trail I'm following."

"Not afraid," said he, and made a gesture to include the whole settlement, then added gently, "No good to fight; the best man will get the most deer anyhow."

And the end of it was that Yan stayed for several days with Chaska, and got, not an antlered buck indeed, but, better far, an insight into the ways of a man who could hunt. The Indian taught him not to follow the trail over the hills, for deer watch their back track, and cross the hills to make this more easy. He taught him to tell by touch and smell of sign just how far ahead they are, as well as the size and condition of the deer, and not to trail closely when the game is near. He taught him to study the wind by raising his moistened finger in the air, and Yan thought, "Now I know why a deer's nose is always moist, for he must always watch the wind." He showed Yan how much may be gained at times by patient waiting, and that it is better to tread like an Indian with foot set straight, for thereby one gains an inch or two at each stride and can come back in one's own track through deep snow. And he also unwittingly taught him that an Indian cannot shoot with a rifle, and Natty Bumpo's adage came to mind, "A white man can shoot with a gun, but it ain't accordin' to an Injun's gifts."

Sometimes they went out together and sometimes singly. One day, while out alone, Yan had followed a deer-track into a thicket by what is now called Chaska Lake. The sign was fresh, and as he sneaked around there was a rustle in the brush. Then he saw the kinnikinnick boughs shaking. His gun flew up and covered the spot. As soon as he was sure of the place he meant to fire. But when he saw the creature as a dusky moving form through the twigs, he awaited a better view, which came, and he had almost pulled the trigger when his hand was stayed by a glimpse of red, and a moment later out stepped--Chaska.

"Chaska," Yan gasped, "I nearly did for you."

For reply the Indian drew his finger across the red handkerchief on his brow. Yan knew then one reason why a hunting Indian always wears it; after that he wore one himself.

One day a flock of prairie-chickens flew high overhead toward the thick Spruce Woods. Others followed, and it seemed to be a general move. Chaska looked toward them and said, "Chickens go hide in bush. Blizzard to-night."

It surely came, and the hunters stayed all day by the fire. Next day it was as fierce as ever. On the third day it ceased somewhat, and they hunted again. But Chaska returned with his gun broken by a fall, and after a long silent smoke he said:

"Yan hunt in Moose Mountain?"

"No!"

"Good hunting. Go?"

Yan shook his head.

Presently the Indian, glancing to the eastward, said, "Sioux tracks there to-day. All bad medicine here." And Yan knew that his mind was made up. He went away and they never met again, and all that is left of him now is his name, borne by the lonely lake that lies in the Carberry Hills.

VI

"There are more deer round Carberry now than ever before, and the Big Stag has been seen between Kennedy's Plain and the mill." So said a note that reached Yan away in the East, where he had been chafing in a new and distasteful life. It was the beginning of the hunting season, the fret was already in his blood, and that letter decided him. For a while the iron horse, for a while the gentle horse, then he donned his moosehide wings and flew as of old on many a long, hard flight, to return as so often before.

Then he heard that at a certain lake far to the eastward seven deer had been seen; their leader a wonderful buck.

With three others he set out in a sleigh to the eastward lake, and soon found the tracks--six of various sizes and one large one, undoubtedly that of the famous Stag.

How utterly the veneer was torn to tatters by those seven chains of tracks! How completely the wild paleolithic beast stood revealed in each of the men, in spite of semi-modern garb, as they drove away on the trail with a wild, excited gleam in every eye!

It was nearly night before the trail warmed up, but even then, in spite of Yan's earnest protest, they drove on in the sleigh. And soon they came to where the trail told of seven keen observers looking backward from a hill, then an even sevenfold chain of twenty-five-foot bounds. The hunters got no glimpse at all, but followed till the night came down, then hastily camped in the snow.

In the morning they followed as before, and soon came to where seven spots of black, bare ground showed where the deer had slept.

Now when the trail grew warm Yan insisted on hunting on foot. He trailed the deer into a great thicket, and knew just where they were by a grouse that flew cackling from its farther side.

He arranged a plan, but his friends would not await the blue-jay's 'all-right' note, and the deer escaped. But finding themselves hard pressed, they split their band, two going one way and five another. Yan kept with him one, Duff, and leaving the others to follow the five deer, he took up the twofold trail. Why? Because in it was the great broad track he had followed for two years back.

On they went, overtaking the deer and causing them again to split. Yan sent Duff after the doe, while he stuck relentlessly to the track of the famous Stag. As the sun got low, the chase led to a great half-wooded stretch, in a country new to him; for he had driven the Stag far from his ancient range. The trail again grew hot, but just as Yan felt sure he soon would close, two distant shots were heard, and the track of the Stag as he found it then went off in a fear-winged flight that might keep on for miles.

Yan went at a run, and soon found Duff. He had had two long shots at the doe. The second he thought had hit her. Within half a mile they found blood on the trail; within another half-mile the blood was no more seen and the track seemed to have grown very large and strong. The snow was drifting and the marks not easily read, yet Yan knew very soon that the track they were on was not that of the wounded doe, but was surely that of her antlered mate. Back on the trail they ran till they solved the doubt, for there they learned that the Stag, after making his own escape, had come back to change off: an old, old trick of the hunted whereby one deer will cleverly join on and carry on the line of tracks to save another that is too hard pressed, while it leaps aside to hide or fly in a different direction. Thus the Stag had sought to save his wounded mate, but the hunters remorselessly took up her trail and gloated like wolves over the slight drip of blood. Within another short run they found that the Stag, having failed to divert the chase to himself, had returned to her, and at sundown they sighted them a quarter of a mile ahead mounting a long snow-slope. The doe was walking slowly, with hanging head and ears. The buck was running about as though in trouble that he did not understand, and coming back to caress the doe and wonder why she walked so slowly. In another half-mile the hunters came up with them. She was down in the snow. When he saw them coming, the great Stag shook the oak-tree on his brow and circled about in doubt, then fled from a foe he was powerless to resist.

As the men came near the doe made a convulsive effort to rise, but could not. Duff drew his knife. It never before occurred to Yan why he and each of them carried a long knife. The poor doe turned on her foes her great lustrous eyes; they were brimming with tears, but she made no moan. Yan turned his back on the scene and covered his face with his hands, but Duff went forward with the knife and did some dreadful, unspeakable thing, Yan scarcely knew what, and when Duff called him he slowly turned, and the big Stag's mate was lying quiet in the snow, and the only living thing that they saw as they quit the scene was the great round form bearing aloft the oak-tree on its brow as it haunted the nearer hills.

And when, an hour later, the men came with the sleigh to lift the doe's body from the crimsoned snow, there were large fresh tracks about it, and a dark shadow passed over the whitened hill into the silent night.

* * * * *

What morbid thoughts came from the fire that night! How the man in Yan did taunt the glutted brute! Was this the end? Was this the real chase? After long weeks, with the ideal alone in mind, after countless blessed failures, was this the vile success--a beautiful, glorious, living creature tortured into a loathsome mass of carrion?

VII

But when the morning came the impress of the night was dim. A long howl came over the hill, and the thought that a wolf was on the trail that he was quitting smote sadly on Yan's heart. They all set out for the settlement, but within an hour Yan only wanted an excuse to stay. And when at length they ran onto the fresh track of the Sandhill Stag himself, the lad was all ablaze once more.

"I cannot go back--something tells me that I must stay--I must see him face to face again."

The rest had had enough of the bitter frost, so Yan took from the sleigh a small pot, a blanket, and some food, and left them, to follow alone the great sharp imprint in the snow.

"Good-by--good luck!"

He watched the sleigh out of sight, in the low hills, and then felt as he never had before. Though he had been so many months alone in the wilds, he had never known loneliness, but as soon as his friends were gone he was overwhelmed by a sense of the utter heart-sickening dreariness of the endless, snowy waste. Where were the charms that he had never failed to find until now? He wanted to recall the sleigh, but pride kept him silent.

In a little while it was too late, and soon he was once more in the power of that fascinating, endless chain of tracks,--a chain begun years ago, when in a June the track of a mother Blacktail was suddenly joined by two little ones' tracks. Since then the three had gone on winding over the land the trail-chains they were forging,--knotted and kinked, and twisted with every move and thought of the makers, imprinted with every hap of their lives, but interrupted never wholly. At times the tracks were joined by that of some fierce foe and the kind of mark was changed, but the chains went on for months and years, now fast, now slow, but endless, until some foe more strong joined on and there one trail was ended. But this great Stag was forging still that mystic chain. A million roods of hills had he overlaid with its links, had scribbled over in this oldest script with the story of his life. If only our eyes were bright enough to follow up that twenty thousand miles of trail, what light unguessed we might obtain where the wisest now are groping!

But skin deep, man is brute. Just a little while ago we were mere hunting brutes--our bellies were our only thought, that telltale line of dots was the road to food. No man can follow it far without feeling a wild beast prickling in his hair and down his spine. Away Yan went, a hunter-brute once more, all other feelings swamped.

Late that day the trail, after many a kink and seeming break, led into a great dense thicket of brittle, quaking asp. Yan knew that the Stag was there to lie at rest. The deer went in up-wind, of course. His eyes and ears would watch his trail, and his nose would guard in front, so Yan went in at one side, trusting to get a shot. With a very agony of care he made his way, step by step, and, after many minutes, surely found the track, still leading on. Another lengthy crawl, with nerves at tense, and then the lad thought he heard a twig snapped behind him, though the track was still ahead. And after long he found it true. Before lying down the Stag had doubled back, and while Yan had thought him still ahead, he was lying far behind, so had gotten wind of the man and now was miles away.

Once more into the unknown north away, till cold, black night came down; then Yan sought out a sheltered spot and made a tiny, red-man's fire. As Chaska had taught him long ago--'Big fire for fool.'

When the lad curled up to sleep he felt a vague wish to turn three times like a dog, and a well-defined wish that he had fur on his face and a bushy tail to lay around his freezing hands and feet, for it was a night of northern frost. Old Peboan was stalking on the snow. The stars seemed to crackle, so one could almost hear. The trees and earth were bursting with the awful frost. The ice on a near lake was rent all night by cracks that went whooping from shore to shore; and down between the hills there poured the cold that burns.

A prairie-wolf came by in the night, but he did not howl or treat Yan like an outsider now. He gave a gentle, doglike 'Woof, woof,' a sort of 'Oho! so you have come to it at last,' and passed away. Toward morning the weather grew milder, but with the change there came a driving snow. The track was blotted out. Yan had heeded nothing else, and did not know where he was. After travelling an aimless mile or two he decided to make for Pine Creek, which ought to lie southeastward. But which way was southeast? The powdery snow was driven along through the air, blinding, stinging, burning. On all things near it was like smoke, and on farther things, a driving fog. But he made for a quaking asp grove, and there, sticking through the snow, he found a crosier golden-rod, dead and dry, but still faithfully delivering its message, 'Yon is the north.' With course corrected, on he went, and, whenever in doubt, dug out this compass-flower, till the country dipped and Pine Creek lay below.

There was good camping here, the very spot indeed where, fifteen years before, Butler had camped on his Loneland Journey; but now the blizzard had ceased, so Yan spent the day hunting without seeing a track, and he spent the night as before, wishing that nature had been kinder to him in the matter of fur. During that first lone night his face and toes had been frozen and now bore burning sores. But still he kept on the chase, for something within had told him that the Grail was surely near. Next day a strange, unreasoning guess sent him east across the creek in a deerless-looking barren land. Within half a mile he came on dim tracks made lately in the storm. He followed, and soon found where six deer had lain at rest, and among them a great, broad bed and a giant track that only one could have made. The track was almost fresh, the sign unfrozen still. "Within a mile," he thought. But within a hundred yards there loomed up on a fog-wrapped hillside five heads with ears regardant, and at that moment, too, there rose up from the snowy top a great form like a blasted trunk with two dead boughs still on. But they had seen him first, and before the deadly gun could play, six beacons waved and a friendly hill had screened them from its power.

The Sandhill Stag had gathered his brood again, yet now that the murderer was on the track once more, he scattered them as before. But there was only one track for Yan.

At last the chase led away to the great dip of Pine Creek--a mile-wide flat, with a long, dense thicket down the middle.

"There is where he is hiding and watching now, but there he will not rest," said the something within, and Yan kept out of sight and watched; after half an hour a dark spot left the willow belt and wandered up the farther hill. When he was well out of sight over the hill Yan ran across the valley and stalked around to get the trail on the down-wind side. He found it, and there learned that the Stag was as wise as he--he had climbed a good lookout and watched his back trail, then seeing Yan crossing the flat, his track went swiftly bounding, bounding--.

The Stag knew just how things stood; a single match to a finish now, and he led away for a new region. But Yan was learning something he had often heard--that the swiftest deer can be run down by a hardy man; for he was as fresh as ever, but the great Stag's bounds were shortening, he was surely tiring out, he must throw off the hunter now, or he is lost.

He often mounted a high hill to scan the white world for his foe, and the after-trail was a record of what he learned or feared. At last his trail came to a sudden end. This was a mystery until long study showed how he had returned backward on his own track for a hundred yards, then bounded aside to fly in another direction. Three times he did this, and then passed through an aspen thicket and, returning, lay down in this thicket near his own track, so that in following, Yan must pass where the Stag could smell and hear him long before the trail brought the hunter over-close.

All these doublings and many more like them were patiently unravelled and the shortening bounds were straightened out once more till, as daylight waned, the tracks seemed to grow stale and the bounds again grow long. After a little, Yan became wholly puzzled, so he stopped right there and spent another wretched night. Next day at dawn he worked it out.

He found he had been running the trail he had already run. With a long hark-back, the doubt was cleared. The desperate Stag had joined onto his old track and bounded aside at length to let the hunter follow the cold scent. But the join-on was found and the real trail read, and the tale that it told was of a great Stag wearing out, too tired to eat, too scared to sleep, with a tireless hunter after.

VIII

A last long follow brought the hunt back to familiar ground--a marsh-encompassed tract of woods with three ways in. There was the deer's trail entering. Yan felt he would not come out there, for he knew his foe was following. So swiftly and silently the hunter made for the second road on the down-wind side, and having hung his coat and sash there on a swaying sapling, he hastened to the third way out, and hid. After a while, seeing nothing, Yan gave the low call that the jaybird gives when there's danger abroad in the woods.

All deer take guidance from the jay, and away off in the encompassed woods Yan saw the great Stag with wavering ears go up a high lookout. A low whistle turned him to a statue, but he was far away with many a twig between. For some seconds he stood sniffing the wind and gazing with his back to his foe, watching the back trail, where so long his enemy had been, but never dreaming of that enemy in ambush ahead. Then the breeze set the coat on the sapling a-fluttering. The Stag quickly quit the hillock, not leaping or crashing through the brush,--he had years ago got past that,--but silent and weasel-like threading the maze, he disappeared. Yan crouched in the willow thicket and strained his every sense and tried to train his ears for keener watching. A twig ticked in the copse that he was in. Yan slowly rose with nerve and sense at tightest tense, the gun in line--and as he rose, there also rose, but fifteen feet away, a wondrous pair of bronze and ivory horns, a royal head, a noble form behind it, and face to face they stood, Yan and the Sandhill Stag. At last--at last, his life was in Yan's hands. The Stag flinched not, but stood and gazed with those great ears and mournful, truthful eyes, and the rifle leaped but sank again, for the Stag stood still and calmly looked him in the eyes, and Yan felt the prickling fading from his scalp, his clenched teeth eased, his limbs, bent as to spring, relaxed and manlike stood erect.

'Shoot, shoot, shoot now! This is what you have toiled for,' said a faint and fading voice, and spoke no more.

But Yan remembered the night when he, himself run down, had turned to face the hunting wolves, he remembered too that night when the snow was red with crime, and now between him and the other there he dimly saw a vision of an agonizing, dying doe, with great, sad eyes, that only asked, 'What harm have I done you?' A change came over him, and every thought of murder went from Yan as they gazed into each other's eyes--and hearts. Yan could not look him in the eyes and take his life, and different thoughts and a wholly different concept of the Stag, coming--coming--long coming--had come.

* * * * *

"Oh, beautiful creature! One of our wise men has said, the body is the soul made visible; is your spirit then so beautiful--as beautiful as wise? We have long stood as foes, hunter and hunted, but now that is changed and we stand face to face, fellow-creatures looking in each other's eyes, not knowing each other's speech--but knowing motives and feelings. Now I understand you as I never did before; surely you at least in part understand me. For your life is at last in my power, yet you have no fear. I knew of a deer once, that, run down by the hounds, sought safety with the hunter, and he saved it--and you also I have run down and you boldly seek safety with me. Yes! you are as wise as you are beautiful, for I will never harm a hair of you. We are brothers, oh, bounding Blacktail! only I am the elder and stronger, and if only my strength could always be at hand to save you, you would never come to harm. Go now, without fear, to range the piney hills; never more shall I follow your trail with the wild wolf rampant in my heart. Less and less as I grow do I see in your race mere flying marks, or butcher-meat. We have grown, Little Brother, and learned many things that you know not, but you have many a precious sense that is wholly hidden from us. Go now without fear of me.

"I may never see you again. But if only you would come sometimes and look me in the eyes and make me feel as you have done to-day, you would drive the wild beast wholly from my heart, and then the veil would be a little drawn and I should know more of the things that wise men have prayed for knowledge of. And yet I feel it never will be--I have found the Grail. I have learned what Buddha learned. I shall never see you again. Farewell."

Ernest Thompson Seton

Born
August 14, 1860
South Shields, England, United Kingdom

Died
October 23, 1946 (aged 86)
Seton Village, New Mexico, United States

Other names
"Ernest Evan Thompson", "Ernest Seton Thompson", "Black Wolf", "Chief"

Occupation
author, wildlife artist

Known for
founder of the Woodcraft Indians and founding pioneer of the Boy Scouts
of America

Awards
John Burroughs Medal (1927)
Daniel Giraud Elliot Medal (1928)
Silver Buffalo Award

Ernest Thompson Seton (August 14, 1860 – October 23, 1946) was an
author (published in the United Kingdom, Canada, and the US), wildlife
artist, founder of the Woodcraft Indians, and one of the founding pioneers
of the Boy Scouts of America (BSA). Seton also influenced Lord Baden-
Powell, the founder of Scouting. His notable books related to Scouting
include The Birch Bark Roll and The Boy Scout Handbook. He is
responsible for the appropriation and incorporation of what he believed to
be American Indian elements into the traditions of the BSA.

Early life

Ernest Thompson Seton, born Ernest Evan Thompson[1] in South Shields,
County Durham (now part of South Tyneside, Tyne and Wear), England of
Scottish parents, Seton's family emigrated to Canada in 1866. Most of his
childhood was spent in Toronto. As a youth, he retreated to the woods to
draw and study animals as a way of avoiding his abusive father. He won a
scholarship in art to the Royal Academy in London, England.[2]

On his twenty-first birthday, Seton's father presented him with a bill for all
the expenses connected with his childhood and youth, including the fee
charged by the doctor who delivered him. He paid the bill, but never spoke
to his father again.[3][4]

Ernest changed his name to Ernest Thompson Seton, believing that Seton had been an important family name. He became successful as a writer, artist and naturalist, and moved to New York City to further his career. Seton later lived at Wyndygoul, an estate that he built in Cos Cob, a section of Greenwich, Connecticut. After experiencing vandalism by the local youth, Seton invited them to his estate for a weekend where he told them what he claimed were stories of the American Indians and of nature.[5]

He formed the Woodcraft Indians in 1902 and invited the local youth to join. Despite the name, the group was made up of non-native boys and girls. The stories became a series of articles written for the Ladies Home Journal, and were eventually collected in The Birch Bark Roll of the Woodcraft Indians in 1906.

Scouting

Seton met Scouting's founder, Lord Baden-Powell, in 1906. Baden-Powell had read Seton's book, The Birch Bark Roll of the Woodcraft Indians, and was greatly intrigued by it. The pair met and shared ideas. Baden-Powell went on to found the Scouting movement worldwide, and Seton became the president of the committee that founded the Boy Scouts of America (BSA) and was its first (and only) Chief Scout. The position of Chief Scout was removed, and the position "Chief Scout Executive" was taken on by James West. His Woodcraft Indians (a youth organization), combined with the early attempts at Scouting from the YMCA and other organizations, and Daniel Carter Beard's Sons of Daniel Boone, to form the BSA.[6] The work of Seton and Beard is in large part the basis of the Traditional Scouting movement.[7]

Seton was Chief Scout of the BSA from 1910–1915 and his work is in large part responsible for the appropriation and incorporation of what he believed to be American Indian elements into the traditions of the BSA.

However, he had significant personality and philosophical clashes with Beard and James E. West.

In addition to disputes about the content of Seton's contributions to the Boy Scout Handbook, conflicts also arose about the suffrage activities of his wife, Grace Gallatin Seton Thompson, and his British citizenship. The citizenship issue arose partly because of his high position within BSA, and the federal charter West was attempting to obtain for the BSA required its board members to be United States citizens. Seton drafted his written resignation on January 29, 1915, but he did not send it to BSA until May.[8]

Personal life

Seton married twice. His first marriage was to Grace Gallatin in 1896. Their only daughter, Ann, was born in 1904 and died in 1990. Ann, who later changed her first name, became a best-selling author of historical and biographical novels as Anya Seton. According to Ann's introduction to the novel Green Darkness, Grace was a practicing Theosophist. Ernest and Grace divorced in 1935, and Ernest soon married Julia M. Buttree. Julia would write works by herself and with Ernest. They did not have any biological children, but did adopt an infant daughter, Beulah (Dee) Seton (later Dee Seton Barber), in 1938. Dee Seton Barber, a talented embroiderer of articles for synagogues such as Torah mantles, died in 2006.

Writing and later life

Seton was an early pioneer of the modern school of animal fiction writing, his most popular work being Wild Animals I Have Known (1898), which contains the story of his killing of the wolf Lobo. He later became involved in a literary debate known as the nature fakers controversy, after John Burroughs published an article in 1903 in the Atlantic Monthly attacking writers of sentimental animal stories. The controversy lasted for four years and included important American environmental and political figures of the day, including President Theodore Roosevelt.[9]

In 1907, Seton and the naturalist Edward Alexander Preble verified a claim from ten years earlier by the frontiersman Charles "Buffalo" Jones that Jones and his hunting party of musk oxen had shot and fended off a hungry wolf pack near the Great Slave Lake in Canada. Seton and Preble discovered the remains of the animals near Jones's long abandoned cabin.[10]

For his work, Lives of Game Animals, Volume 4, Seton was awarded the Daniel Giraud Elliot Medal from the National Academy of Sciences in 1928 .[11] In 1931, he became a United States citizen. Seton was associated with the Santa Fe arts and literary community during the mid-1930s and early 1940s, which comprised a group of artists and authors including author and artist Alfred Morang, sculptor and potter Clem Hull, painter Georgia O'Keeffe, painter Randall Davey, painter Raymond Jonson, leader of the Transcendental Painters Group, and artist Eliseo Rodriguez.[12] He was made a member of the Royal Canadian Academy of Arts.[13]

He died in Seton Village in northern New Mexico at the age of eighty-six. Seton was cremated in Albuquerque. In 1960, in honor of his 100th birthday and the 350th anniversary of Santa Fe, his daughter Dee and his grandson, Seton Cottier (son of Anya), scattered the ashes over Seton Village from an airplane.[14]

Legacy

The Philmont Scout Ranch houses the Seton Memorial Library and Museum. Seton Castle in Santa Fe, built by Seton as his last residence, housed many of his other items. Seton Castle burned down in 2005; fortunately all the artwork, manuscripts, books, etc., had been removed to storage before renovation was to have begun.[15]

The Academy for the Love of Learning, an educational organization in

Santa Fe, acquired Seton Castle and its contents in 2003. The new Academy Center opened in 2011 includes a gallery and archives featuring artwork and other materials as part of its Seton Legacy Project. The Seton Legacy Project organized a major exhibition on Seton opening at the New Mexico History Museum on May 23, 2010, the catalog published as Ernest Thompson Seton: The Life and Legacy of an Artist and Conservationist by David L. Witt.

Roger Tory Peterson drew inspiration for his field guide from the simple diagram of ducks that Seton included in Two Little Savages.[16]

Several of Seton's works are written from the perspective of a predator and were an influence upon Robert T. Bakker's Raptor Red.[17]

Seton is honoured by the Ernest Thompson Seton Scout Reservation in Greenwich, Connecticut, USA, and with the E.T. Seton Park in Toronto, Canada. Obtained in the early 1960s as the site of future Metro Toronto Zoo, the land was later used to establish parkland and home to the Ontario Science Centre. Seton is mentioned in Philip Roth's Novel, "Nemesis," where he is credited for having introduced Indian Lore to the American Camping movement.[18]